LEGENDS OF WARFARE
AVIATION

P-38 Lightning, Vol. 1

Lockheed's XP-38 to P-38H in World War II

DAVID DOYLE

SCHIFFER MILITARY

4880 Lower Valley Road   Atglen, PA 19310

Designed by Justin Watkinson
Type set in Impact/Minion Pro/Univers LT Std

ISBN: 978-0-7643-5659-9
Printed in China

Published by Schiffer Publishing, Ltd.
4880 Lower Valley Road
Atglen, PA 19310
Phone: (610) 593-1777; Fax: (610) 593-2002
E-mail: Info@schifferbooks.com
www.schifferbooks.com

For our complete selection of fine books on this and related subjects, please visit our website at www.schifferbooks.com. You may also write for a free catalog.

Schiffer Publishing's titles are available at special discounts for bulk purchases for sales promotions or premiums. Special editions, including personalized covers, corporate imprints, and excerpts, can be created in large quantities for special needs. For more information, contact the publisher.

We are always looking for people to write books on new and related subjects. If you have an idea for a book, please contact us at proposals@schifferbooks.com.

Acknowledgments

As with all of my projects, this book would not have been possible without the generous help of many friends. Instrumental to the completion of this book were Tom Kailbourn, Rich Kolasa, Dana Bell, Stan Piet, and Scott Taylor, as well the staff and volunteers at the National Museum of the United States Air Force. Most importantly, I am grateful for the help and support of my wife, Denise.

Contents

Introduction

Perhaps no aircraft design is more iconic than that of the P-38 Lightning. In spite of the passage of seven decades, its distinctive silhouette remains immediately recognizable. Over 10,000 of the iconic aircraft were built, with production encompassing a dozen models. This volume will explore the early variants, while volume 2 will examine the later models.

The P-38 was a collaboration of two of America's most notable aircraft designers: Hall Hibbard and Clarence "Kelly" Johnson. Johnson's name is well known by aviation enthusiasts for other iconic aircraft such as the P-80, F-104, U-2, and SR-71. In February 1937, as the US Army Air Corps was soliciting proposals for a new pursuit aircraft, Johnson was serving as Hibbard's assistant. Soon they would embark on the design that was to eventually become the Lightning.

One of the more remarkable facts about the Lightning is that it was the only US pursuit-type (P-) aircraft that would remain in continuous production throughout World War II. This is no small feat given the swift development of aircraft design and the changing doctrine of air warfare. The Lightning also suffered from rather inauspicious beginnings; neither the prototype XP-38 nor the first service-test (YP-38) aircraft survived their testing phase.

The Air Corps distributed "Specification X-608" to aircraft manufacturers in early 1937. This document laid out various criteria to potential designers. Among them was the desire for an aircraft with a top speed of 360 mph that could climb to 20,000 feet in six minutes. Also required was sufficient fuel capacity to fly at full throttle for one hour. Among the recipients was Lockheed, where Hibbard and Johnson conceptualized several dual-engine aircraft. The final concept would be Lockheed's first pursuit-type aircraft.

Prior to the introduction of the P-38, the Curtiss P-36 Hawk was the basis for the US pursuit aircraft. The prototype of the type first flew in May 1935, and deliveries of the standardized P-36A began in April 1938. Produced in multiple variants, the aircraft was exported to a number of countries, including Great Britain and France. Although obsolete compared to other nations' aircraft by the time the US entered World War II, several Hawks sortied during the Pearl Harbor attack and managed to shoot down two Japanese Zeros, at a loss of one of their own. *National Museum of the United States Air Force*

Considerably impressed with the potential shown by the turbosupercharged, liquid-cooled Allison V-1710 engine, in early 1937 the Army Air Corps contracted with Curtiss to modify one P-36 to Allison power. The resultant aircraft, designated the XP-37, had a streamlined cowling and propeller spinner. Radiators were mounted on the sides of the cowl, and the cockpit was shifted aft compared to that of the P-36. Ultimately, while the Army ordered thirteen YP-37 service test aircraft, for the Curtiss airframe they favored an Allison with mechanically driven supercharger, an aircraft known as the P-40. The turbosupercharged Allison used in the YP-37 would soon be adapted to Lockheed's XP-38. *National Museum of the United States Air Force*

Much of the basis for Hibbard and Johnson's choice of a twin-engine design was the need to meet the Army's requirements for top speed and rate of climb. The distinctive twin-boom layout provided considerable stability. Each of the housings contained a portion of the tricycle landing gear. They also housed the turbosuperchargers that were essential to the high-altitude performance of the Allison V-1710 twelve-cylinder engines. Mounted between the booms, the center fuselage was unencumbered by an engine. This created a space for a cluster of weaponry directly ahead of the pilot, making aiming simply a matter of pointing the aircraft at its intended target.

Another innovation was the use of butt-jointed, flush-riveted skin, which added significant streamlining.

Lt. Benjamin Kelsey of Wright Field's Pursuit Projects Office was impressed with the design, which is notable since he was the author of Specification X-608. Lt. Kelsey recommended that the Air Corps obtain an aircraft for tests, and on June 23, 1937, Air Corps Contract 9974 was awarded for one XP-38. The resultant aircraft, Air Corps serial number 37-457, would cost a mere $163,000—not an insubstantial amount at the time, but very low when compared to more-modern projects.

The design phase took one year, and even before that work was complete, manufacture of the prototype began in Burbank, California. Teams of skilled Lockheed workers assembled the prototype, in secrecy, since the aircraft remained highly classified.

During construction, another innovation was added to the design: that of contrarotating engines. This allowed the torque of the two engines to be canceled out, eliminating control problems both at takeoff and landing.

After assembly, XP-38 was subjected to a battery of initial checks. Once passed, it was now time to get the design airborne. At that point it was partially dismantled and prepared for road shipment. On New Year's Eve 1938, the aircraft began the 62-mile journey by truck from Burbank to Riverside, California. This was the location of a remote World War I airbase known as March Field. Upon arrival, the big fighter was reassembled and ground tests were performed.

Lt. Ben Kelsey now played another role in the birth of the Lightning. Because Lockheed had no test pilots on its payroll at that time, Lt. Kelsey served in that capacity. Kelsey, who was to eventually rise to the rank of brigadier general, was well qualified. He had a master's degree in engineering from MIT and was also an experienced test pilot. The XP-38 lifted into the air on its maiden flight on January 27, 1939.

Due to the remarkable performance of the XP-38, Lt. Kelsey began thinking of ways to exploit it. On February 11, he was scheduled for a ferry flight from March Field to the Air Corps test center at Wright Field, near Dayton, Ohio. He had hoped to set a Los Angeles–Dayton speed record during this trip, and en route Kelsey noted that the aircraft was making remarkably good time, arriving in Amarillo, Texas, for refueling after only two hours and forty-eight minutes. The next leg of Amarillo to Dayton took only two hours and forty-five minutes. Gen. Henry H. "Hap" Arnold, chief of the Army Air Corps, met Kelsey and the XP-38 at the field. After conferring with Arnold, Kelsey decided to refuel and fly on to New York, in an attempt to beat Howard Hughes's cross-country speed record established just two years before.

During the approach to Mitchel Field, Long Island, the carburetor air intakes of the XP-38 iced up and the aircraft lost power. This caused it to come in short of the runway, and it crashed onto the Cold Stream Golf Course. Although Kelsey survived, the aircraft was destroyed—as was the record set by Mr. Hughes—besting it by some twenty minutes of air time.

Because of the significant potential shown by the design, on April 27, 1939, the Air Corps ordered thirteen service-test aircraft. The "Y" in their YP-38 designation would indicate their use.

In June 1937, Lockheed received a contract to produce one XP-38 prototype. This plane, assigned US Army Air Corps serial number 38-326, is viewed from the front left. The overall lines of the plane are similar to the production P-38s, with some details differing, such as the lack of fixed oil-cooler intakes on the chins of the engine nacelles and the presence of air scoops on the tops of those nacelles. *National Museum of the United States Air Force*

The XP-38 had a retractable oil-cooler air intake on the bottom of each engine nacelle; the one on the left nacelle is visible a few feet to the rear of the propeller. The XP-38 had an Allison V-1710-11 turbosupercharged engine on the left and a V-1710-15 on the right; the engines' shafts operated in different directions, with the propellers rotating toward the inboard part of the plane at the tops of their rotations. *National Museum of the United States Air Force*

On the top of each of the tail booms of the XP-38 was a swiveling exhaust duct, a feature that distinguished this plane from the YP-38s, which lacked this duct. Both ducts are open in this photograph. The first flight for the XP-38 was on January 27, 1939; the pilot on that occasion was Lt. Benjamin Kelsey.
National Museum of the United States Air Force

A large contingent of civilians, probably Lockheed employees, are gathered around the XP-38 as it is being fueled at Wright Field, Ohio, prior to taking off on a record-breaking cross-country flight from March Field, California, to Mitchel Field, Long Island, in February 1939. One of the men atop the plane is leaning on the top panel of the cockpit canopy, which was hinged on the right side.
National Museum of the United States Air Force

Lockheed test and Army Lt. Benjamin S. Kelsey, in the flight suit and helmet, is standing on the right wing of the XP-38. *National Museum of the United States Air Force*

During Ben Kelsey's cross-country flight in the XP-38, he was about to land at his final destination at Mitchel Field, Long Island, on February 11, 1939, when one of the carburetors iced up, leading to engine failure. He belly-landed the plane on a golf course and walked away from the plane uninjured. However, the XP-38 was beyond repair. *National Museum of the United States Air Force*

CHAPTER 2
YP-38

The next step in the evolution of the P-38 was the YP-38. Lockheed's internal designation was Model 122. Development of the aircraft took eighteen months, during which time Lockheed expanded its Burbank facilities.

Significant changes were made to the power plant of the YP-38. Twin 1,150-horsepower Allison V-1710-27/-29 (F2R/F2L) engines with B-2 turbosuperchargers and spur reduction gearing replaced the V-1710-11 and 15 of the prototype, which caused the engine's thrust line to be raised.

The propellers now rotated outward rather than inward as on the XP-38. Although this reduced tail buffeting, it made single-engine operation challenging.

A pair of cooling intakes replaced the retractable oil and intercooler intake under each prop spinner, along with large radiator scoops added on the sides of each boom. This would become a characteristic feature on the production model P-38.

The first YP-38 went airborne on September 16, 1940, with Marshall Headle at the controls. Delivery of the first YP-38 was in March 1941, with the final YP-38 completed in June.

Severe tail buffeting plagued the aircraft at speeds near Mach 0.68. This was especially acute in dives, making pullout difficult. During a test flight in November 1941, a tail boom failure of the first YP-38 cost test pilot Ralph Virden his life.

Extensive testing revealed the failure to be due to the shifting of the center of lift as airflow increased, although the Army had believed that the tail booms had come off as a result of flutter.

The Army Air Corps received thirteen examples of the service-test model of the Lightning, the YP-38, or Lockheed Model 122-62-02. The first flight for the YP-38 was on September 16, 1940, and the last of the YP-38s was completed in June 1941. The power plant consisted of an Allison V-1710-27 and a V-1710-29; these drove the propellers in opposite directions, as was the case with the YP-38, except the YP-38 propellers spun away from the center of the aircraft at the top of their rotations. *Air Force Historical Research Agency*

A YP-38 is viewed from below during flight. This service-test version of the Lightning featured new, larger housings for the radiators on the tail booms. On the side of the left tail boom, below the trailing edge of the wing, is a carburetor-air scoop. *National Archives*

A test pilot is putting a Lockheed YP-38 through its paces. On the center of the rudder is a mass balance, a feature that was added to the top and the bottom of the rudder to reduce tail buffeting.
Air Force Historical Research Agency

The first YP-38, serial number 39-689 and Lockheed construction number 122-2202, is viewed from above on a tarmac. This plane crashed after the tail separated from the aircraft during a high-speed dive over Glendale, California, on November 4, 1941; the test pilot, Ralph Virden, was killed. *National Museum of the United States Air Force*

The first YP-38 is viewed from above and to the front with a pilot at the controls. This plane had a single-piece canopy and a rounded control yoke. The propellers were Curtiss Electrics with cuffs on the blades. *National Museum of the United States Air Force*

This YP-38 is equipped with a three-piece windscreen with two vertical frame members on the front, similar to the design used on the British Lightning Mk. 1 and the first production model of US Lightnings, the P-38-LO. No weapons were mounted in the noses of the YP-38s. A close view of the photo shows that a round headrest was mounted on a frame above the top of the pilot's seat. *National Museum of the United States Air Force*

Fake machine gun barrels have been mounted on the nose of YP-38 serial number 39-692. There are two vertical splitter plates in the center of the oil-cooler air inlet in the chin of the left engine nacelle; this was to divide the airflow to the two oil coolers inside the nacelle. Early production models of the Lightning would have two separate inlets for the oil coolers, and these inlets would be circular when viewed from the front. *Air Force Historical Research Agency*

Five YP-38s are parked at the Lockheed facility at Burbank, California. Although YP-38s had nomenclature and serial number stencils on the left sides of the pilot's nacelles, as the fuselage of the P-38 sometimes was referred to, and occasionally had their construction numbers painted on their noses, YP-38s generally were photographed without markings that would help in identifying them. *Air Force Historical Research Agency*

A Lockheed YP-38 flies over a city, presenting a sleek, streamlined vision of things to come with future, production P-38s. Despite the fatal crash of the first YP-38, the service-test YP-38s performed well during evaluations and would form the foundation for successive models of Lightnings. *National Museum of the United States Air Force*

A Lockheed YP-38 flies high above a desert landscape. Note the pitot tube on a mast below the nose, the two vertical frames on the windscreen, and the two mass balances on the top and the bottom of the center of the elevator. *Air Force Historical Research Agency*

CHAPTER 3
P-38

In general, the first model of production Lockheed Lightnings, the P-38-LO, was similar to the YP-38s, with the P-38-LOs also being equipped with pilot armor and bullet-resistant glass. The first of the P-38-LOs, serial number 40-744 and tail number 0744, is seen here, painted in Olive Drab over Neutral Gray camouflage and fitted with a light-colored patch with dummy machine gun barrels on the nose. The P-38-LOs were not normally armed, but when they were built it was anticipated that the P-38s would have four .50-caliber machine guns and a 37 mm aircraft cannon. *National Museum of the United States Air Force*

The Army simply designated the first production model of the new twin-boom aircraft P-38. Lockheed's internal designation was Model 222. Modern historians often use the term "P-38-LO," in order not to confuse it with the generic P-38-type (LO representing Lockheed's Burbank facility).

The initial performance of aircraft so impressed the Army that production of the P-38 began while the YP-38 was still undergoing testing.

Twenty-nine aircraft were produced (some sources say 30), with the first one delivered in June 1941, and the last in August.

The nineteenth P-38 produced, serial number 40-762, was completed as a P-38A. Uniquely, it featured a pressurized cockpit. Army Air Force serial numbers assigned to the twenty-nine P-38s were 40-744 through 40-761 and 40-763 through 40-773,

corresponding to Lockheed construction numbers 222-2215 through 222-2232 and 222-2234 through 222-2244.

The projected armament for the P-38 was four .50-caliber machine guns and a 37 mm cannon, although it was not typically installed. Armor protection and bullet-resistant glass were installed in the cockpit. The Lightning was slowly becoming a more combat-worthy aircraft, but there would be many more changes in store before it was truly combat capable.

Interestingly, in keeping with Lockheed's tradition of selecting aircraft names from mythological characters, the P-38 was initially known as the "Atalanta," after the Greek goddess. To lasting effect, when the British ordered the subsequent Model 322 they assigned it the name "Lightning."

A Western Air Express hangar is in the background of this right-rear view of a P-38-LO. This model of Lightning still had the original large air scoop to the front of each turbosupercharger, atop the engine nacelles. *National Museum of the United States Air Force*

The landing gear and the Fowler flaps of a P-38-LO are lowered as the plane approaches an airfield for a landing. A very small number "18" is painted on the side of the nose. *National Museum of the United States Air Force*

Lockheed P-38-LO, serial number 40-791, is secured to a ferry consisting of a platform attached to two DUKW amphibious trucks. There are openings for guns in the nose, and, curiously, the large air-intake scoops on top of the engine nacelles, forward of the turbosuperchargers, have been replaced by panels with small air scoops, similar to those encountered on later models of the P-38.
National Museum of the United States Air Force

Early-model Lockheed P-38s are under assembly at the Lockheed plant at Burbank, California. These Lightnings have natural-metal finish (note the highly polished propeller spinners and pilot's nacelles) and the prewar national insignia with the red circle in the center. The noses have been perforated for the installation of guns. *Jim Gilmore collection*

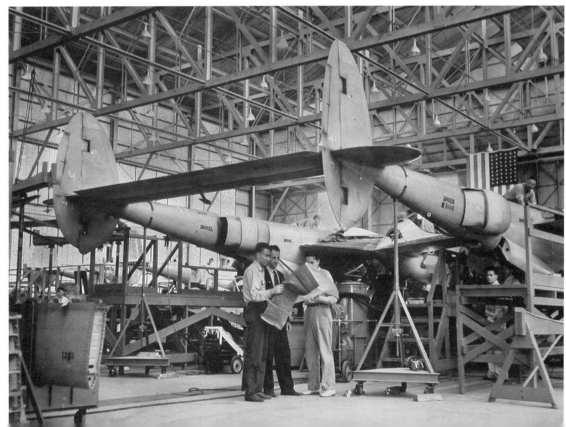

Lockheed workers review blueprints between the twin booms of an early-model P-38 Lightning. *Jim Gilmore collection*

CHAPTER 4
P-322

The British contracted for 143 examples of the Lockheed Lightning, designated the Model 322-B and dubbed the Lightning I. The Lightning Is were powered by Allison V-1710-C15 engines without turbosuperchargers, so performance, especially at high altitudes, suffered as a result. After receiving and evaluating three examples of this aircraft, the British canceled the remainder of the order. Shown here is one of the Lightning Is, in British camouflage and insignia.
Stan Piet collection

As war swept across Europe, both France and England looked to augment their native aircraft-manufacturing capabilities by purchasing aircraft built in the United States. The big Lightning caught the attention of both nations. In April 1940, the Anglo-French Purchasing Committee placed orders for 667 Lightnings, each nation ordering aircraft in its own unique configurations.

Designated the Model 322-B for the British and Model 322-F for the French, the aircraft bore Lockheed model numbers 322-61-03 for the English, and 322-61-04 for the French.

Because both countries intended to use the aircraft at low levels, they viewed the turbosupercharger as an expensive, complicated, and unnecessary component. Further, the units were in short supply and thus apt to delay delivery of the badly needed aircraft.

Additionally, both nations required that the aircraft be equipped only with Allison V-1710-C15 right-hand-rotation engines, as opposed to the counterturning engines used on other Lightnings.

The French-bound aircraft had French radios, instruments, and controls, including notably throttles that were of the French configuration, which operated opposite of that of US aircraft.

After the Fall of France, Great Britain took over both orders, designating the aircraft Lightning I.

Soon, however, after contractual disputes with Lockheed, the British canceled all but 143 of the Lightning Is.

With the US entry into World War II, the US Army Air Forces (USAAF) agreed to take all of the Lightning I aircraft canceled by the British. The Army Air Force retained the original engine configuration on twenty-two of the aircraft, designating them P-322-I. These aircraft were used for testing and training. The remaining 121 aircraft, designated the P-322-II or RP-322-II (the R prefix, standing for "Restricted to noncombat use"), were modified to use counterrotating engines by installing Allison V-1710-27 and V-1710-27M, F-2, engines. These aircraft were used primarily as advanced trainers.

Upon the US entry into World War II, the US Army Air Forces assumed custody of the 140 Lightning I aircraft from the order canceled by the British. These aircraft were redesignated the P-322. Twenty-two examples with non-counterrotating propellers were designated P-322-I and were used for testing and training purposes, and the remainder, modified for counterrotating propellers, were designated P-322-II (or, eventually, RP-322-II, when the plane was pronounced restricted from combat use). The P/RP-322IIs served as advanced trainers, and some were armed with two .50-caliber and two .30-caliber machine guns. Seen here at Shreveport, Louisiana, in January 1943 is RP-322-II, serial number AF103. *Stan Piet collection*

A Lockheed RP-322-I prepares for a mission at Chico Army Airfield, California. The serial number, AF207, is prominently displayed on the nose, cowling, and bottom of the wing. Note the different-colored propeller spinners as well as the round headrest for the pilot; there is no armor behind the headrest. *Stan Piet collection*

The engines of Lockheed P-322, serial number AF110, are being run up with the wheels chocked and the top panel of the right cowling removed. Although the plane is unarmed, faintly visible to the front of the windscreen is a bead sight. *National Museum of the United States Air Force*

This aircraft, serial number AE979, was the second plane that was to have been a Lightning I. Although it is painted in British camouflage and bears British roundels and fin flashes, the plane was never accepted by the Brits. Instead, it served as a P-322 in American service; it was scrapped at San Bernardino, California, on November 13, 1945. *National Museum of the United States Air Force*

This P-322 still retains its original RAF serial number, AF196. In USAAF service, this aircraft was assigned to a training squadron, and it was scrapped at Williams Field, Arizona, in November 1945. Note the covers on the tires. *National Museum of the United States Air Force*

An example of an RP-322-II was serial number AF132, seen at a desert air base. A characteristic of the P-322-II was the inclusion of counterrotating propellers coupled to Allison V-1710F-2 engines. Stenciled below the "AF132" on the nose is "RP-322" and a semilegible notice on fuel-octane requirements for this aircraft. *National Archives*

CHAPTER 5
P-38D

The final sixty-six P-38-LOs received modifications intended to make the aircraft combat capable, although in reality these planes, designated P-38D-LO, failed to attain that status. They had a low-pressure oxygen system, a retractable landing light, self-sealing fuel tanks, and improvements to reduce buffeting and enhance recovery after a dive. This example with dummy gun barrels and the nickname "Snuffy" on the nose bears the red cross pertaining to the Red Force during the Carolina Maneuvers in late 1941. *Stan Piet collection*

All thirty-six P-38Ds were converted from the final portions of the P-38 production. The aircraft were delivered from August to October 1941 and were assigned USAAF serial numbers 40-774 to 40-809. These aircraft were eventually to be classified RP-38D, R being the designation for "Restricted to non-combat use."

In order to alleviate tail buffeting, fillets were installed around the joint between the leading edge of the wing and the central nacelle joint. The fairings for the wing / central nacelle joint were fitted to later P-38Ds. These had been originally installed on the British Lightning I.

Typically, armament was four .50-caliber machine guns mounted nonsymmetrically. A 37 mm cannon was projected, but both weapons were rarely installed.

During P-38D production, 37 mm aircraft cannon were in extremely short supply. Because of this shortage, beginning with the P-38E, Lightnings were armed with the 20 mm Hispano-Suiza cannon.

It was hoped that the addition of self-sealing fuel tanks and a low-pressure oxygen system to the P-38D would make it fit for combat, but the Army still did not find it satisfactory for that use.

The P-38D was not to see much frontline service; rather, it was used as a test bed for improvements to the P-38 series. It did have an important role as a training and familiarization aircraft. Both pilots and ground crews needed to get accustomed to this innovative new aircraft.

Members of the 1st Pursuit Group received several of the P-38D models to supplement their P-38s. Both types of aircraft were flown in the fall 1941 Louisiana Maneuvers, providing them with much-needed expertise.

A P-38D-LO with dummy gun barrels on the nose has a white cross signifying the Blue Force during the Carolina Maneuvers in late 1941. The plane is chocked and secured to stakes in the ground to prevent wind damage. *National Museum of the United States Air Force*

The P-38Ds lacked the cross-bracing on the roll-down side panels of the canopy and the lateral brace on the hinged top panel of the canopy; these features would be introduced with the P-38F model. *National Museum of the United States Air Force*

Aside from the national insignia, the only marking visible on this P-38D is a small number "45" painted on the side of the nose. *National Museum of the United States Air Force*

The same P-38D, marked with the number "45" in small figures on the sides of the nose, is viewed from the front. The 20 mm cannon is not mounted; its opening is visible at the center of the .50-caliber machine gun array. The Curtiss Electric propeller blades are unpainted metal. *National Museum of the United States Air Force*

During Army experiments to assess the effects on pilots in cockpits offset from the centerline of aircraft, the first P-38D-LO, serial number 40-744, was converted to a test plane. A cockpit with a bubble canopy was installed in the left boom, and the turbosuperchargers were omitted from both sides of the plane. *National Museum of the United States Air Force*

CHAPTER 6
P-38E

The P-38E-LO was another step toward a genuinely combat-ready Lightning (although this model too failed to fully reach that goal). A total of 210 P-38E-LOs were completed. Some of the changes over the P-38D included the deletion of the large air scoops to the fronts of the turbosuperchargers, in favor of smaller scoops; a revamped nose landing gear with a smaller gear bay; more space for machine gun ammunition; and staggered .50-caliber machine guns in the nose. A 20 mm cannon also was included in the armaments package. This P-38E-LO has "86E" marked on the cowling and a faint construction number, which appears to be 5504, on the nose. If that is the case, this plane was serial number 41-2286, the sixth-from-last P-38E completed. *Air Force Historical Research Agency*

At first glance, the P-38E appeared identical to the P-38D. However, internally there were more than 2,000 changes to the design. The aim of the engineering team was to create the first truly combat-ready Lightning.

A total of 210 P-38Es were produced at Lockheed's Burbank plant. They were delivered between October 1941 and February 1942. Lockheed assigned its model number 222-62-09.

The power plant of the P-38E remained the Allison V-1710-27 and V-1710-29, F-2, turbosupercharged engines, rated at 1,150 horsepower each.

Notable external changes included a retractable landing light mounted under the left wing and the addition of improved instruments and hydraulic and electrical systems. Another innovation, first applied to the Lightning I / P-322 series, was that the drag strut of the nose landing gear was moved to the rear. This permitted the main nose gear strut to be shortened, resulting in the nose landing gear requiring less space. Consequently, the gun bay was redesigned, doubling the ammunition capacity.

The P-38E now featured four .50-caliber Colt-Browning MG 53-2 machine guns installed in the nose, with staggered barrels.

P-38E Lightnings made their first kills of enemy aircraft in the Aleutian Islands on August 4, 1942. That day, Lt. Kenneth Ambrose and Lt. Stanley Long, of the 54th Fighter Squadron, claimed two Japanese H6K "Mavis" flying boats.

Action in the Aleutians highlighted shortcomings in the cockpit-heating system. The engine typically heated fighters of that time. In most aircraft designs, this was just ahead of the cockpit. However, heating the remote cockpit of the P-38 was problematic given the distance from the aircraft's twin engines.

The ninety-nine F-4-1 reconnaissance aircraft were based on the P-38E airframe design. They were given Lockheed model number 222-62-13. The F-4s were purpose built on the assembly line for their role as reconnaissance aircraft, unlike later conversions from fighter aircraft.

A P-38E-LO with the aircraft number "52" on the tail and the nose is viewed from below in flight. A noticeable change from preceding models of the Lightning is the new fillet between the leading edge of the wing and the side of the pilot's nacelle, or fuselage. This feature was part of measures taken to reduce tail flutter. *Air Force Historical Research Agency*

The last two digits of this P-38E-LO's serial number, 41-2014, are painted in black on the cowling. On the nose is the plane's construction number, 5232. Note the oval polished-metal mirror on the inboard side of the left cowling: this was a standard item that enabled the pilot to visually ascertain the position of the landing gear.
Air Force Historical Research Agency

The P-38E cockpit featured the early-style control wheel, which described two-thirds of a circle. The wheel was mounted on an L-shaped control column. The box on the right spoke of the wheel contained the triggers for the 20 mm cannon (facing the camera) and the .50-caliber machine guns (out of view on the front of the box). The rudder trim-tab control crank and oxygen controls are on the center console on floor, with rudder pedals to its sides. On the left side of the cockpit are controls for throttles, fuel mixture, propellers, landing gear, and other systems. At the top is a flat piece of bullet-resistant glass. *National Museum of the United States Air Force*

Lockheed construction number 5468 is stenciled on the side of the nose of this P-38E-LO; this number coincides with USAAF serial number 41-2250. The national insignia is the pre–May 1942 style with the red circle in the center. *National Museum of the United States Air Force*

At one time, the concept of converting P-38s to floatplanes was explored. For that purpose, P-38E, serial number 41-1986, was modified with uplifted tail booms. The tail booms curved upward from the rears of the radiator housings, and their cross sections were thicker than those of stock P-38Es, with a fairly sharp bottom edge. No production floatplanes resulted from these experiments. *National Museum of the United States Air Force*

Lockheed converted P-38E-LO, serial number 41-2048, to an experimental aircraft to evaluate means of streamlining the aircraft. The pilot's nacelle extended aft of its normal length, the original cockpit became an observer's cockpit, and a new pilot's cockpit was installed farther forward. A test boom was mounted on the nose. A lightning bolt was painted on the pilot's nacelle, and the construction number, 5266, is painted on the nose. *National Museum of the United States Air Force*

P-38E-LO, serial number 41-2048, was equipped with laminar-flow wings. Spraying equipment for airflow studies was mounted aft of the left outboard section of laminar-flow wing. *National Museum of the United States Air Force*

CHAPTER 7
F-4

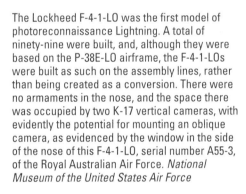

The Lockheed F-4-1-LO was the first model of photoreconnaissance Lightning. A total of ninety-nine were built, and, although they were based on the P-38E-LO airframe, the F-4-1-LOs were built as such on the assembly lines, rather than being created as a conversion. There were no armaments in the nose, and the space there was occupied by two K-17 vertical cameras, with evidently the potential for mounting an oblique camera, as evidenced by the window in the side of the nose of this F-4-1-LO, serial number A55-3, of the Royal Australian Air Force. *National Museum of the United States Air Force*

The P-38F featured numerous minor improvements over its predecessor, the P-38E, and was the first Lightning to be produced in multiple production blocks. The blocks are identified as the P-38F-LO (quantity = 126), P-38F-1-LO (151), P-38F-5-LO (100), P-38F-13-LO (29), and P-38F-15-LO (121), for a total of 527 aircraft. The P-38F-13-LO and P-38F-15-LO were originally British Lightning IIs.

Three identification lights (red, blue-green, and amber, front to back) were installed toward the lower rear of the central nacelle, and a fixed tab was incorporated into each aileron. Engines were changed to the Allison V-1710-49 and V-1710-53, each rated at 1,325 horsepower.

The P-38F saw the significant introduction of external fuel tanks. The center wing section was strengthened and two pylons were installed that permitted the carrying of two tanks (or bombs up to 1,000 pounds each).

The tanks came in two sizes, 75 and 165 gallons, with the latter being designed by Kelly Johnson. This tank was to be adapted later for use with several other aircraft. Although they effectively doubled the fuel capacity and significantly increased the aircraft's range, the large tanks also created performance problems. Certain maneuvers could not be accomplished with the tanks in place. Since the tanks did not have fuel gauges, it was difficult to determine exactly when they were nearing empty, in order to release them. It was found that the empty tanks could not be safely dropped at speeds over 160 mph. Full tanks could be released at speeds up to 400 mph.

Twenty F-4A-1 reconnaissance aircraft were produced at the same time as the P-38F. These differed from the previous F-4-1 in that cameras could be mounted obliquely as well as vertically in their noses.

The cockpit of an F-4-1-LO is viewed from the right side. To the front of the pilot's seat is an intervalometer, for controlling the intervals between the taking of the reconnaissance photographs. On the upper-right spoke of the control wheel is a box containing the camera start-and-stop control button. *National Museum of the United States Air Force*

CHAPTER 8
P-38F

The P-38F featured numerous minor improvements over its predecessor, the P-38E, and was the first Lightning to be produced in multiple production blocks. The blocks are identified as the P-38F-LO (quantity = 126), P-38F-1-LO (151), P-38F-5-LO (100), P-38F-13-LO (29), and P-38F-15-LO (121), for a total of 527 aircraft. The P-38F-13-LO and P-38F-15-LO were originally British Lightning IIs.

Three identification lights (red, blue-green, and amber, front to back) were installed toward the lower rear of the central nacelle, and a fixed tab was incorporated into each aileron. Engines were changed to the Allison V-1710-49 and V-1710-53, each rated at 1,325 horsepower.

The P-38F saw the significant introduction of external fuel tanks. The center wing section was strengthened and two pylons were installed that permitted the carrying of two tanks (or bombs up to 1,000 pounds each).

The tanks came in two sizes, 75 and 165 gallons, with the latter being designed by Kelly Johnson. This tank was to be adapted later for use with several other aircraft. Although they effectively doubled the fuel capacity and significantly increased the aircraft's range, the large tanks also created performance problems. Certain maneuvers could not be accomplished with the tanks in place. Since the tanks did not have fuel gauges, it was difficult to determine exactly when they were nearing empty, in order to release them. It was found that the empty tanks could not be safely dropped at speeds over 160 mph. Full tanks could be released at speeds up to 400 mph.

Twenty F-4A-1 reconnaissance aircraft were produced at the same time as the P-38F. These differed from the previous F-4-1 in that cameras could be mounted obliquely as well as vertically in their noses.

The fold-down step is in the lowered position below the rear of the pilot's nacelle of P-38F-13-LO, serial number 43-2044. The number "97" is stenciled on the side of the nose. *National Museum of the United States Air Force*

A P-38F is viewed from the front at an unidentified airfield. This plane likely was P-38F-1-LO, serial number 41-7632, seen in the two following photographs. *National Museum of the United States Air Force*

Lockheed P-38F-1-LO, serial number 41-7632, is seen from the left front. On the nose is a faded and illegible construction number as well as the remnants of a larger and equally illegible number. The construction number for this plane was 5759, so it is likely that the larger number on the nose, following the common practice of painting the last two digits of a construction number in that position, was "59," which is in keeping with what is visible of that larger number. *National Museum of the United States Air Force*

The left side of P-38F-1-LO, serial number 41-7632, is displayed. Beginning with the P-38F, the pitot tube was moved from the nose to the bottom of the left wing, and an SCR-552-A antenna was installed on the bottom of the nose to the front of the nose landing gear. *National Museum of the United States Air Force*

This final view of P-38F-1-LO, serial number 41-7632, shows the plane from the left rear. This Lightning was used for aerodynamics research at the National Advisory Committee for Aeronautics (NACA), Ames Aeronautical Laboratory, at Naval Air Station Moffett Field, California, from December 1942 to July 1943. *National Museum of the United States Air Force*

This stunning in-flight close-up shows P-38F-1-LO, tail number 17586 and serial number 41-7586. Aircraft number "15" is marked on the nose and above the tail number. The SCR-552-A radio antenna is clearly visible below the nose. The gun barrels are wrapped with masking tape for protection from the elements. *National Museum of the United States Air Force*

A P-38F marked with the number "68" on the tail is carrying two 165-gallon drop tanks. The main landing-gear doors are in the open position. *National Museum of the United States Air Force*

The only identification marking on this P-38F, aside from the national insignia, is the number "47" on the nose. The lower mass balance on the rudder is clearly visible in silhouette. *National Museum of the United States Air Force*

Lockheed P-38F-1-LO, serial number 41-7630 and construction number 222-5757, was assigned to the 94th Fighter Squadron, 1st Fighter Group, in 1942. On July 15 of that year, during a ferrying flight to Great Britain, this plane, along with five other Lightings and two B-17s, was forced to make an emergency landing on an ice sheet in Greenland. During the ensuing decades, an accumulation of almost 270 feet of snow and ice buried the plane. In 1992, a half century after its emergency landing, the plane was excavated by the Greenland Expedition Society. Later, the Lightning was transported to Middlesboro, Kentucky, where it was painstakingly restored to flying condition. Since then, it has flown under the nickname "Glacier Girl," painted in blue with white outlining on the nose. *Rich Kolasa*

After a decade of restoration work, "Glacier Girl" made her first public flight on October 26, 2002. Since then, thousands of spectators have witnessed the plane in flight at air shows. The restored Lightning incorporated approximately 80 percent of its original parts and components. Since 2006, "Glacier Girl" has been part of the collections of Lewis Air Legends. *Rich Kolasa*

"Glacier Girl" bears the tail number 17630, an abbreviation of its serial number, 41-7630, and the number in yellow on the nose, 5757, is an abbreviation of its construction number, 2220-5757. The national insignia is the type with the red circle in the center, authorized through May 6, 1942, but retained on many US Army Air Forces aircraft for up to several months after that date. *Rich Kolasa*

The original Allison engines of "Glacier Girl" were replaced by remanufactured Allison engines during the aircraft's restoration. The plane is painted in standard USAAF camouflage of Olive Drab over Neutral Gray. *Rich Kolasa*

The civil registration number of "Glacier Girl," NX17630, is marked in black on the lower part of the vertical fin, below the horizontal stabilizer. The "Glacier Girl" nickname is not repeated on the right side of the nose. *Rich Kolasa*

"Glacier Girl" is viewed from the right rear while taxiing at an airport. Note the radiator housing on the side of the boom just aft of the national insignia, and the two teardrop-shaped mass balances on the top and the bottom of the elevator. *Rich Kolasa*

Matte dark-blue covers are on the main landing-gear wheels of "Glacier Girl," as seen in an overall view of the plane from the left side. *Rich Kolasa*

The nose landing gear is turned hard right in this frontal view of "Glacier Girl" with the Allison engines running. The two round intakes for the oil coolers of the left engine are visible on the lower front of the left cowling. *Rich Kolasa*

A close-up of the nose of "Glacier Girl" shows the barrels of the four .50-caliber Browning M2 machine guns and, below them, the single Hispano AN-M2C 20 mm cannon. The machine guns in the restored aircraft are functional. *Author photo*

Two ejector ports for spent .50-caliber cartridge cases, marked with stencils "SHELL EJECTION," are on the right side of the pilot's nacelle (or fuselage) above the nose landing-gear door. The interiors of the ports are bare metal, and a bare-metal air deflector is at the front of each port. *Author photo*

The forward parts of the barrels of three of the .50-caliber machine guns and the AN-M2C 20 mm cannon are seen from the right side. The actual .50-caliber gun barrels are only as thick as the chrome muzzles; over the barrels are perforated cooling sleeves. The vented muzzle of the 20 mm cannon is painted Olive Drab. *Author photo*

The nose landing gear of "Glacier Girl" is observed from the right side, showing the relative position of the two right spent-casing ejector ports. *Author photo*

The nose landing gear is seen from the front, including the oleo strut and the torque-link "scissor" mechanism. Above the torque link is the nosewheel shimmy damper. When the plane made its emergency landing in Greenland in 1942, the pilot, Lt. Harry Smith, made a wheels-up belly landing that was so smooth, the propeller blades were not bent. Thus, the landing gear was salvageable, although the tires were replaced during the restoration. *Author photo*

The nose landing gear is seen from the right side. Above the wheel shimmy damper is the right lower drag link. The wheel cover is fastened to the wheel with three slotted screws. *Author photo*

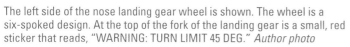

The left side of the nose landing gear wheel is shown. The wheel is a six-spoked design. At the top of the fork of the landing gear is a small, red sticker that reads, "WARNING: TURN LIMIT 45 DEG." *Author photo*

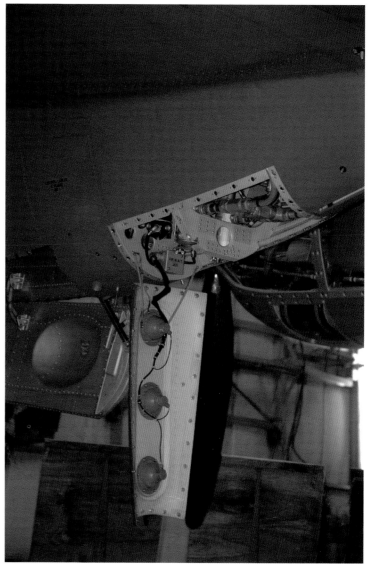

A hinged panel on the belly of the fuselage aft of the nose landing-gear bay provided access to elements of the fuel system. Mounted on the hinged panel are three recognition lights, a feature introduced to Lightnings beginning with the P-38F. *Author photo*

In a view under the left wing, the left retractable landing light and the pitot tube, the latter with a red cover over it, are in view. There was a similar landing light on the bottom of the right wing. P-38s up to the E model had the pitot tube under the nose. *Author photo*

The left main landing-gear bay and its two doors are viewed from the rear, with the nose landing gear faintly visible in the center background, past the jack stand. *Author photo*

A view from next to the right engine nacelle with the cowling panels removed shows the Allison V-1710 engine, as well as the cockpit canopy, windscreen, and pilot's seat. A red "NO STEP" marking is on the top of the frame of the rolled-down right-side window of the cockpit. *Author photo*

More of the right side of the right engine, propeller, and fuselage is shown. Each propeller blade has the Curtiss Electric logo decal, featuring a three-bladed propeller, as well as a yellow data stencil. *Author photo*

In a close-up view of the right Allison V-1710 engine, just aft of the propeller spinner is the coolant expansion tank. Below the V-shaped engine support under the engine is the right oil cooler, behind an air duct attached to the air intake on the chin of the engine nacelle. To the upper rear of the engine are the oil tank and turbo air ducts. *Author photo*

The right engine is observed from the front, showing the two air intakes for the oil coolers on the chin, as well as the nacelle frame. *Author photo*

More details of the oil-cooler air intakes are visible; the fronts of the perforated cores of the oil coolers are visible inside the intakes. Under the wing to the left is a jack stand. *Author photo*

The right Allison engine of "Glacier Girl" is displayed, showing the maze of coolant, exhaust, and fuel pipes. *Author photo*

In a view of the two tail booms of "Glacier Girl," the right turbosupercharger is visible in a recess on the top of the near boom. Between the two small turbosupercharger cooling-air scoops to the front of the turbosupercharger is the engine exhaust duct. Engine exhaust gases were what drove the turbosupercharger. *Author photo*

The brass-colored left oil cooler is visible below the left engine of "Glacier Girl." Just aft of the propeller spinner, and above the shielded ignition harness, is the rust-colored exhaust manifold. *Author photo*

The rounded object in the upper rear of the left engine compartment is the oil tank. The two oil tanks of the Lightning were fabricated from 3SO aluminum alloy, and each had a capacity of thirteen gallons, but a total of 8.25 gallons was normally carried during flight operations. *Author photo*

The yellow data stencil on one of the left propeller blades is seen close-up. The small, round hole between the two oil-cooler air intakes is the inlet for the lower engine blast tube. *Author photo*

The bullet-shaped object on the side of the left tail boom of "Glacier Girl" is the carburetor air intake. Farther aft is the boom's left radiator housing. *Author photo*

In a view taken alongside the left propeller spinner, the Olive Drab fixture in the front of the engine compartment is a cooling-air intake for the exhaust manifold and shroud. This intake jutted through the cowling panel when the latter was fastened in place. *Author photo*

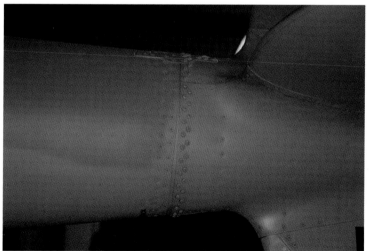

The outboard side of the joint between the left aft tail boom (*left*) and the empennage boom (*right*) is observed close-up. The two sections were mated at station 393 and were fastened together by a mix of flatheaded and roundheaded Phillips screws. A stiffener is attached to the top of the joint. *Author photo*

The lower mass balance of "Glacier Girl" is displayed. It is shaped somewhat like a 165-gallon Lockheed drop tank, as used on P-38s, and is mounted on an airfoil-type pedestal. *Author photo*

The left side of the left tail of "Glacier Girl" is depicted. Above the "7" in the tail number is a clear position light. Below the tail number are three access panels: left to right, there is one panel for the elevator pulleys and two panels for the tab actuator. *Author photo*

The left empennage of "Glacier Girl" is displayed. Below the civil registration number, NX17630, is an access panel for the elevator pulleys. Above the "7" in the tail number is a clear, teardrop-shaped running light. *Author photo*

Once lost to the snows and ice of time, "Glacier Girl" almost miraculously continues to fly, a testament to the endurance and excellent construction of the P-38s and to the dedication and expertise of the persons who recovered and restored the plane. *Rich Kolasa*

CHAPTER 9
P-38G

A wartime color photo shows Lockheed P-38G-10-LO, serial number 42-3519 and construction number 7953, parked at an unidentified airfield. The P-38G differed from its predecessor the P-38F mainly in that it was powered by Allison V-1710-51/55 engines, rather than the F-model's V-1710-49/53 engines. *National Museum of the United States Air Force*

The P-38G was produced in several blocks, and they were broken down as follows: P-38G-1-LO (quantity = 80), P-38G-3-LO (12), P-38G-5-LO (68), P-38G-10-LO (548), P-38G-13-LO (174), and P-38G-15-LO (200). The blocks totaled 1,082. Lockheed model numbers 222-68-12 were assigned to blocks P-38G-1 through P-38G-10. Model numbers 322-60-19 went to blocks P-38G-13 and P-38G-15. This was to eliminate a discrepancy in blocks P-38G-13 and P-38G-15 after they were ordered by the British as Lightning IIs.

The inboard wing sections began to be further reinforced with the P-38G-10-LO. This was accomplished in order to help bear the weight of an underwing-mounted 2,000-pound bomb or 300-gallon drop tank, the latter being for long-range ferrying.

Even though the drop tanks provided a notable advantage to the range of the aircraft, they were considered highly hazardous to jettison in flight, and they were not used in combat. Instructions were given to drop them only in an emergency. With the extension of range, the low-pressure oxygen system was also upgraded to match the extended flight time.

The P-38G was produced on contract number 21217, which was issued in October 1941 and was valued at $108,914,000.00. More than 1,000 P-38G model units were manufactured—a milestone in Lightning production.

Like many of the other previous models, a photoreconnaissance version of the P-38G was produced. Given the designation F-5A, 180 aircraft were built concurrent with the other aircraft. F-5A production was divided into three groups: twenty F-5A1s, twenty F-5A-3s, and 140 F-5A-10. Lockheed model number 222-68-16 was assigned. Although very similar to the F-4A-1, the internal camera arrangement of the F-5A differed considerably.

This unmarked Lightning exhibits some of the features of the P-38G (and its predecessor, the P-38F): the X-braces on the side windows, the radio mast antenna under the nose, the pitot tube under the left wing, and the wing pylons. *National Museum of the United States Air Force*

The first P-38G-1-LO, serial number 42-12687, is observed from the left side. On the nose, in small figures, is the construction number, 7121; in larger numerals are the last two numbers of the construction number, "21." The construction numbers typically were painted in the same Neutral Gray as the undersides of the Lightnings, and thus these numbers usually appear faint and often illegible in vintage photographs. This plane lacks the radio mast on the bottom of the nose, and a test boom is mounted on the nose. *National Museum of the United States Air Force*

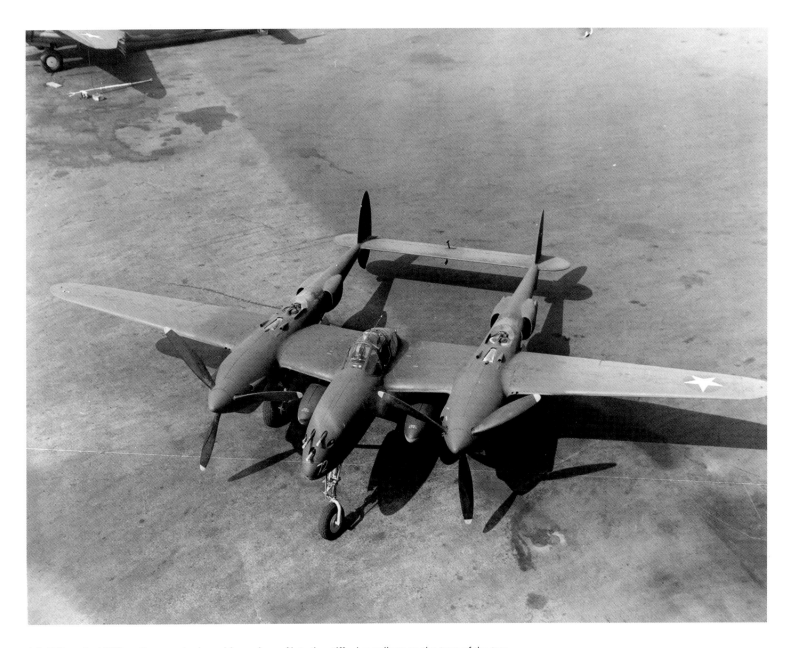

A P-38G marked "72" on the nose is viewed from above. Note the stiffening splines on the tops of the two drop tanks. "NO STEP" warning markings are also on the tops of these tanks.
National Museum of the United States Air Force

This and the following three photos were taken in late December 1942 to document the cockpit of P-38G number 3444. At the top is the bullet-resistant flat plate of glass. Between that glass and the early-style control wheel is the glare shield, which was made of canvas and was snapped to a metal frame. To the lower right is the pilot's seat. *National Museum of the United States Air Force*

The bullet-resistant glass has been removed from its mounting to the rear of the windscreen, revealing the reflector gun sight, to the immediate front center of the lower bracket for the glass. A ring sight is to the left of the gun sight. To the lower right is the top of the control column; to the left are the throttle, propeller, and fuel-mixture controls. Below the main instrument panel are, left, the gun-charging selector and handle, and, right, the main electrical panel. *National Museum of the United States Air Force*

The left side of the cockpit is shown with the pilot's seat removed. Just aft of the throttle controls is a small box with the master control switches for the bombs and the drop tanks. Immediately aft of that box is the hand crank for the side window. The pilot's oxygen hose is to the lower right. *National Museum of the United States Air Force*

The first P-38G-1-LO is viewed from the front. The test probe was offset to the right of center of the nose. *National Museum of the United States Air Force*

The machine gun ports on the nose of the first P-38G-1 were covered with tape, but a single gun barrel is protruding through the tape below the test boom. *National Museum of the United States Air Force*

The first P-38G-1-LO, serial number 42-12687, is seen during a flight, with the test probe not installed on the nose. Tape remains over the machine gun ports on the nose. *National Museum of the United States Air Force*

Experiments were conducted at Ladd Field, Alaska, with a P-38G equipped with a Federal Aircraft retractable ski landing gear in January 1944. The tests, which generally were a success, were to determine if the P-38 could operate adequately from snow-covered airfields in Arctic regions. The plane is seen here taxiing on the skis. *National Museum of the United States Air Force*

P-38G-10-LO, serial number 42-13444 (construction number 222-7878), is warming its engines during testing of the Federal Aircraft ski kit at Ladd Field, Alaska, on January 15, 1944. *National Museum of the United States Air Force*

This P-38G with Federal Aircraft skis made a belly landing on January 15, 1944, when the landing gear failed. This appears to have been a different P-38G than the one in the preceding photo, since what is visible of the construction number on the nose (a "5" is definitely present) is inconsistent with that in the preceding image. *National Museum of the United States Air Force*

The Lockheed F-5A was an unarmed photoreconnaissance plane based on the P-38G airframe. They were equipped with five reconnaissance cameras in the nose for photographing both vertically and obliquely. This F-5A-10-LO, nicknamed "Stinky II," served with the 9th Photographic Reconnaissance Squadron, 9th Bombardment Group, and was photographed in India around late 1943. *National Archives*

An F-5A marked number "71," serving with the 90th Photographic Reconnaissance Wing, is parked inside a stone revetment in North Africa. The camera windows were perfectly flat, and where they were mounted on curved parts of the nose, they were installed on flat, recessed surfaces. *National Archives*

As seen on an F-5A taxiing on a dirt runway in North Africa, the upper-side camera window on the right side of these planes was square and smaller than the quadrilateral side window on the left side of the nose. In addition, this window was lower than the one on the left side. *National Archives*

CHAPTER 11
P-38H

The P-38H differed from the P-38G principally in its more powerful Allison V-1710-89/91 engines, which were rated at 1,425 horsepower: a great improvement over the P-38G's Allison V-1710-51/55 (F-10) engines, which were capable of only 1,325 horsepower on takeoff and 1,150 horsepower at 27,000 feet. The P-38H also had the M2C 20 mm cannon instead of the P-38G's M1, and its pylons had a higher capacity, 1,600 pounds on each one. Shown here, wearing the red-bordered national insignia briefly used in the summer of 1943, is P-38H-5-LO, serial number 42-67079. *Air Force Historical Research Agency*

Like many other weapons in the US arsenal in World War II, design development was based on critical feedback from the troops. Due to reports of reduced engine power above 25,000 feet, Lockheed incorporated automatic shutters for the oil coolers and radiators on the P-38H. A long-standing difficulty was leakage in the intercoolers mounted in the leading edges of the outer wing sections, and this was finally addressed in this design. Additionally, automatic controls were added to the turbosuperchargers. Installation of the improved B-33 turbosuperchargers started with the P-38H-5-LO.

In spite of these changes, further redesign of the coolant system would be required to permit the V-1710-89 and V-1710-91 engines to reach peak performance.

Manufacture of the P-38H saw a change in armament, with the 20 mm M1 cannon replaced by the 20 mm M2C cannon, which had been mounted in the P-38E through G. The M2 receiver was 0.2 inches longer compared to the M1. The receiver of the M1 slide was riveted, compared to the bolted one of the M2. Both guns had the identical rate of fire of 600–700 rounds per minute, with a muzzle velocity of about 2,850 feet per second.

Underwing bomb and drop-tank capacity of the P-38H was improved to 3,200 pounds.

The prototype for the new model was the first P-38H-1-LO. This aircraft, in addition to ten P-38H-1-LO prototypes, made up contract AC-21217. Two production blocks were designated for the P-38H. With the P-38H-1-LO, 226 examples were delivered, including the prototype. The next was P-38H-5-LO, which consisted of 375 aircraft, bringing the total produced to 601.

Oddly, no photoreconnaissance variant of the P-38H was ordered from Lockheed. No official records exist that such aircraft were created in the field.

Ground crewmen and a pilot are checking over a P-38H-1-LO. The construction number on the side of the nose is 1146, which coincided with USAAF serial number 42-66635. The top panel of the canopy is the rear-hinged type introduced during P-38F production. *National Archives*

P-38H-5-LO, serial number 42-67079, is seen from off the left beam during a test flight over the desert. Under the wing is a 165-gallon drop tank. *Air Force Historical Research Agency*

The left engine is stopped and the propeller is feathered during what probably was a manufacturer's test flight of Lockheed P-38H-5-LO, serial number 42-67079, in or around the summer of 1943. The reflective polished-metal oval panel on the inboard side of the right engine nacelle is particularly evident.
Air Force Historical Research Agency

A final photo of P-38H-5-LO, serial number 42-67079, shows the plane from the left front during a summer 1943 test flight over an arid suburban landscape, likely in Southern California. The left engine is still stopped and the propeller is feathered in this view. *Air Force Historical Research Agency*

A Lockheed P-38H-5-LO is carrying 1,000-pound bombs on its pylons. Several color photos were taken on the same occasion of this aircraft in flight. The plane was serial number 42-66923, and the last three digits of that number were painted in large, black numbers on a white oval on the cowling.
Air Force Historical Research Agency

The instrument panel and some of the controls of a P-38H are viewed from the pilot's perspective. Between the throttle levers to the lower left and the bottom left corner of the instrument panel is the gun-charging selector knob and lever. To the bottom right is the control column, with part of the control wheel visible. Above the instrument panel is the gunsight, to the front of the bullet-resistant glass panel. *National Museum of the United States Air Force*

The right side of the gun bay of a P-38H is displayed with the cover open. To the left is the magazine for the 20 mm ammunition. Farther forward are the two right-hand .50-caliber machine guns, in staggered position. On the outboard sides of the machine guns are the ammunition feed chutes, leading down to the ammunition magazines below the machine guns. *Roger Freeman collection*

Specifications

	XP-38	YP-38	P-38	P-38D	P-38E	P-38F	P-38G	P-38H
Armament	none fitted	none fitted	4 x .50-cal. MG + 1 x 37 mm	4 x .50-cal MG	4 x .50-cal. MG + 1 x 20 mm	4 x .50-cal. MG + 1 x 20 mm	4 x .50-cal. MG + 1 x 20 mm	4 x .50-cal. MG + 1 x 20 mm
Bomb load	none	none	none	none	none	2,000 lbs.	4,000 lbs.	4,000 lbs.
Engines (2)	Allison V-1710-11/15, C-9	Allison V-1710-27/29, F-2	Allison V-1710-27/29, F-2	Allison V-1710-27/29, F-2	Allison V-1710-27/29, F-4	Allison V-1710-49/53, F-5	Allison V-1710-51/55, F-10	Allison V-1710-89/91, F-17
Max speed	413 mph @ 20,000 ft.	405 mph @ 20,000 ft.	395 mph @ 20,000 ft.	390 mph @ 20,000 ft.	395 mph @ 20,000 ft.	395 mph @ 25,000 ft.	400 mph @ 25,000 ft.	402 mph @ 25,000 ft.
Cruise speed		330 mph	310 mph	300 mph	300 mph	305 mph	340 mph	250 mph
Service ceiling	38,000 ft.	38,000 ft.	38,000 ft.	39,000 ft.	39,000 ft.	39,000 ft.	39,000 ft.	40,000 ft.
Range	1,390 miles	1,150 miles	1,490 miles	970 miles	975 miles	1,925 miles	2,400 miles	2,400 miles
Wing span	52 ft.	52 ft.	52 ft.	52 ft.	52 ft.	52 ft.	52 ft.	52 ft.
Length	37 ft. 10 in.	37 ft. 10 in.	37 ft. 10 in.	37 ft. 10 in.	37 ft. 10 in.	37 ft. 10 in.	37 ft. 10 in.	37 ft. 10 in.
Height	12 ft. 10 in.	12 ft. 10 in.	12 ft. 10 in.	12 ft. 10 in.	12 ft. 10 in.	12 ft. 10 in.	12 ft. 10 in.	12 ft. 10 in.
Weight	13,964 lbs. gross	13,500 lbs. gross	14,178 lbs. gross	14,456 lbs. gross	14,424 lbs. gross	15,900 lbs. gross	15,800 lbs. gross	16,300 lbs. gross
Number built/converted	1	13	29	36	210 + 99 F-4-1	527 + 20 F-4A-1	1082 + 180 F-5A	601

Three of the P-38D-LOs assigned to the Blue Force in the Carolina Maneuvers are on the flight line at
Randolph Field, outside San Antonio, Texas, in late 1941. These planes have the tails, "1P," for 1st Pursuit
Group, as well as individual aircraft numbers: "54" on the closest Lightning and "51" on the next one.
National Museum of the United States Air Force

On a flight line of P-38Ds of the 1st Pursuit Group at or around the time of the Carolina Maneuvers in late 1941, three airmen stand next to the closest plane while two others sit in the shade under the plane. White crosses are on the noses and the wings of these Lightnings. *National Museum of the United States Air Force*

In a photograph reportedly taken in March 1942, a Lockheed Lightning is stowed on the main deck of a ship for transport overseas. The original label on the photo identifies the plane as a Model 322, but it's not clear if it was a British Lightning I or Lightning II (both of which carried the Model 322 designation), or a US P-322. Evidence of British-style camouflage paint is faintly visible on the aircraft. *Grumman Memorial Park via Leo Polaski*

In a March 1942 photograph possibly related to the preceding one, Lockheed Lightnings with the outer wings detached are stored above the main deck of a tanker ship. On the lower parts of the tails of the two closest planes are data stencils, including "PROJECT" followed by an illegible number. *Grumman Memorial Park via Leo Polaski*

A Lockheed Lightning is parked on a hardstand at Muroc Army Airfield (later, Edwards Air Force Base), California, in March 1942. It is likely that this is the same P38F-LO depicted in the following photograph. Note the light-colored masking tape wrapped around the gun muzzles, to protect the gun bores from foreign objects and the elements. *Library of Congress*

Lockheed P-38F-LO, serial number 41-7511, is viewed from the right side at Muroc Army Air Field, California, in May 1942. Faintly visible on the side of the nose is sketchy artwork, apparently a depiction of an elephant. Muroc was an Army Air Forces flight-testing site. *Library of Congress*

Lockheed P-38F-1-LO Lightning, serial number 41-7580, assigned to the 1st Fighter Group, is parked at a base in England in June 1942. Another Lightning, landing gear raised, is in the air in the background, buzzing the field. *Roger Freeman collection*

A group of Lockheed P-38s from the 27th Fighter Squadron were photographed during an extended layover at a base in Iceland on July 6, 1942. Seven weeks later, the planes would resume their ferry flight to the United Kingdom. At the center is P-38F-1-LO, serial number 41-7598, while to the left is P-38F-1-LO, serial number 41-7540. *National Museum of the United States Air Force*

168829-R

162/7-42-806

Using lines attached to a P-38 Lightning, native dockworkers at an unidentified harbor are steadying the plane as a boom on the ship in the background is lifting it. In the background is a wrecker with a semitrailer coupled to it. Another P-38 is secured to the deck of the ship. This photo is likely related to the following one. *National Archives*

A wrecker is towing a semitrailer with a Lockheed Lightning of unknown model on New Caledonia, in the Pacific, on September 27, 1942. Presumably the plane had arrived by ship at New Caledonia, since the wings are detached, machine guns and cannon are not mounted, and joints in the aluminum skin have been treated with sealant. *National Archives*

A partially disassembled P-38 is being transported on a trailer along a street in an unidentified town, possibly in New Caledonia, judging by the signs in French. The photo was taken in or around September 1942. At the time, the United States armed forces were using New Caledonia as an assembly area for materiel destined for the war in the South Pacific. *National Archives*

A Cletrac high-speed tractor is being put to use towing a damaged P-38 from the 14th Fighter Group at Youks-les-Bains Airfield, in Algeria, during the North Africa Campaign, December 1942. A construction number is very faintly visible on the nose: it appears to be 7008. If so, this plane would be P-38F-5-LO, serial number 42-12574. This plane had been damaged in combat when a German fighter shot-up one of the engines. *National Archives*

Members of the 49th Fighter Squadron, 14th Fighter Group, are making repairs to the left engine on a P-38 Lightning at the Youks-les-Bains Airfield, Algeria, in December 1942. The man to the left is kneeling on a scaffolding platform. Under the oil pan of the engine to the right, an underwing pitot tube is visible: this feature originated with the P-38F. *National Archives*

At the desolate, isolated airfield at Youks-les-Bains, Algeria, in December 1942, P-38F-1-LO, serial number 41-7595, is parked to the left. The code HV-S is marked on the tail boom. Living conditions at the base were rough, with tents being used for quarters, and the original label of this photograph remarked concerning the locale, "A good day, no mud." *National Museum of the United States Air Force*

A P-38F or P-38G with tiger mouths painted on the cowlings is parked in a grassy field on Guadalcanal during 1942. The number "33" is painted on the nose and on the tail. *National Archives*

Ground crewmen prepare P-38E-LO, serial number 41-2239, for its next mission at Longview Airfield, on Adak in the Aleutian Islands in late 1942. This plane was assigned to the 54th Fighter Squadron, 343rd Fighter Group, 11th Air Force. Jack stands are supporting the Lightning, and the nose gear is either retracted or has been removed. *National Archives*

At an airfield on Adak Island in the Aleutians in 1942, pilots of the 11th Air Force are walking out to their P-38 Lightnings prior to a mission. These likely were aircraft and men of the 54th Fighter Squadron, 343rd Fighter Group. The nearest Lightning has a drop tank under its wing. *National Archives*

To the left in this view of Lockheed Lightnings at an airfield in the Aleutians in 1942 is P-38E, serial number 41-2079. The cap of the nose of the P-38 to the right is painted in a light color. *National Museum of the United States Air Force*

At an advanced airbase in Tunisia in late 1942, ground crewmen of the 14th Fighter Group, 12th Air Force, are preparing a P-38 Lightning for its next mission. The plane, numbered "42" on the gun compartment door, has the radio antenna mast under the nose, a feature introduced with the P-38F. Thus, this plane was either a P-38F, P-38G, or P-38H. *Roger Freeman collection*

An F-5A, a photoreconnaissance Lightning based on the P-38G airframe, is warming its engines prior to takeoff at an advanced base in North Africa in late 1942. Two camera windows are visible on the side of the nose, and one is on the bottom of the nose. The plane is equipped with Lockheed-made 165-gallon drop tanks. *National Archives*

A Lockheed F-5A reconnaissance Lightning marked with the number "35" on the nose is flying a mission over farmlands in North Africa toward the end of 1942. *National Archives*

The same F-5A shown in the preceding photo, number "35," is flying over low clouds in a mountainous area of North Africa in late 1942. Lockheed F-5As typically were painted in a camouflage scheme referred to as Synthetic Haze. A yellow border was painted around the national insignia. *National Archives*

Capt. Robert L. Faurot of the 39th Fighter Squadron, 35th Fighter Group, poses next to his P-38F-3-LO, serial number 42-12623, at Schwimmer Air Base, Laloki, New Guinea, on January 20, 1943. The numeral "1" in the large number "16" on the nose partially hides the construction number stenciled on the nose, but what is visible is consistent with the correct construction number, 7057. Capt. Faurot was credited with the first kill of an enemy plane by a P-38 in the Pacific theater, when a bomb he released in preparation for engaging Japanese fighters exploded, destroying a fighter. He was shot down in this plane and killed in action during the Battle of the Bismarck Sea on March 2, 1943. *National Archives*

A P-38H-1-LO nicknamed "Pluto," serial number 42-66683, is being serviced between missions at an unidentified base in the South Pacific. To the left, the crew chief, Sgt. Willard Berg, is reviewing a form. SSgt. William Visocan and Cpl. Dan Collins are working on the plane. A single rising-sun flag adjacent to the number "208" on the nose represents the shooting down of a Japanese plane. The nose art is of the Disney character "Pluto." *National Archives*

A P-38 Lightning assigned to the 2nd Service Group warms its engines preparatory to takeoff at Camp Tripoli, Iceland, on March 16, 1943. Only part of the tail number is visible: the first number, "2," and the last three numbers, "596." This tail number was consistent with that of a P-38F or a P-38H, but since the H model did not go into service until May 1943, this plane is thought to have been P-38F-5-LO, serial number 42-12596. *National Museum of the United States Air Force*

These two P-38 Lightning pilots, 2nd Lts. Harry R. Stengle and James M. McNulty Jr., from the 50th Fighter Squadron, based at Keflavik, Iceland, received joint credit for shooting down a German Junkers Ju 88 bomber on a reconnaissance mission near Reykjavik on April 24, 1943. In this publicity photo taken on May 2, 1943, Stengle and McNulty are walking away from one of the two Lightnings that shot down the Ju 88. The number on the nose, 7037, is the suffix of the plane's construction number, 222-7037: this pertained to a P-38F-5-LO. *National Archives*

An armorer standing on a ladder reloads the .50-caliber machine guns of a P-38H from the 38th Fighter Squadron while another ground crewman prepares to place a parachute pack on the pilot's seat, at RAF Nuthampstead, England, on October 16, 1943. On the tip of the nose is a small, round aperture for the gun camera. *National Archives*

Pilot Arthur N. Rowley of the 20th Fighter Group poses with his P-38 Lightning at a base in England in October 1943. The number "1550" is faintly visible on the nose: this refers to construction number 222-1550, which pertains to a P-38H-5-LO. *Roger Freeman collection*

During aerial combat over Treasury Island in the Solomon Islands on October 7, 1943, a Japanese 20 mm shell struck the left engine of this P-38, nicknamed "Jan II," from the 339th Fighter Squadron, 12th Fighter Group. The landing gear was incapacitated, forcing the pilot, Lt. D. W. Livsey, to make a crash landing at Barakoma Field, on Vella Lavella. Livsey survived the landing. Here, two men look over the wreckage of the plane. The guns already have been salvaged from the plane. The number on the nose, 1404, refers to this aircraft's construction number, which pertained to a P-38H-5-LO, serial number 42-66893.
National Archives

"Flying Wolf" was the nickname of P-38H-5-LO, serial number 42-67020, flown by Maj. Milton Joel, commanding officer of the 38th Fighter Squadron, 55th Fighter Group. The nose art, portraying a light-gray P-38 with a wolf's head in place of the pilot's nacelle, superimposed over a white circle with a thin red border, was painted by Sgt. Robert Sand, who also snapped this photograph. Eleven days after this photo was taken, Maj. Joel was shot down and killed in action while flying "Flying Wolf" on November 29, 1943. *Roger Freeman collection*

Lockheed P-38G-10-LO, serial number 42-12962, was photographed during the time it was piloted by Capt. Harry J. Dayhuff, of the 82nd Fighter Squadron. The name "Mackie" painted in script on the gun compartment door was the nickname of Dayhuff's wife. "MIKE" was painted aft of the number "10" on the right cowling. The photo was taken before the 82nd Fighter Squadron transitioned to P-47s in February 1943. *National Museum of the United States Air Force*

The pilot of a Lightning, probably a P-38H, coded CG-B, of the 38th Fighter Squadron, 55th Fighter Group, VIII Fighter Command, has just started the engines. The photo was taken sometime before April 1944, when the 38th Fighter Squadron began flying P-51s. An interesting detail is the round screen spaced slightly ahead of the front of the carburetor air intake on the side of the boom, to keep out foreign objects. *Roger Freeman collection*

A ground crewman is giving hand signals to the pilot taxiing a P-38 Lightning from the 55th Fighter Group. The squadron/aircraft code on the tail boom is faint but appears to be CG-B, which is the same code as on the P-38H in a preceding photo, which was with the 38th Fighter Squadron, 55th Fighter Group.
Roger Freeman collection

Capt. Donald H. McAuley of the 20th Fighter Group confers with his crew chief following his first combat mission in December 1943. The plane was a P-38H5-LO, serial number 42-67081, nicknamed "Pistol Packin' Mama." A glimpse of the risqué nose art is to the left. *Roger Freeman collection*

A thin layer of snow coats the top of the nearest of two Lightnings on a hardstand at a base, probably Nuthampstead, England, P-38H-5-LO, serial number 42-67077, and squadron/aircraft code CG-Q. It was assigned to the 38th Fighter Squadron, 55th Fighter Group, and was nicknamed "Mountain Ayers," a takeoff on the name of the pilot, Capt. Jerry H. Ayers. This plane was shot down, resulting in the death of pilot 1st Lt. William K. Birch, during a mission against Bremen, Germany, on December 16, 1943.
Roger Freeman collection

Col. John "Jack" S. Jenkins, commander of the 55th Fighter Group, poses next to his plane, a P-38H-1-LO, serial number 42-67074, and nicknamed "Texas Ranger," at RAF Nuthampstead in October 1943. Subsequently, Col. Jenkins flew three P-38Js, nicknamed "Texas Ranger II" through "Texas Ranger IV," and he was flying number IV when shot down by flak over France on April 10, 1944. Jenkins became a prisoner of war, but he survived World War II. *Roger Freeman collection*